Nomad Press

A division of Nomad Communications

10 9 8 7 6 5 4 3 2 1

Copyright © 2019 by Nomad Press. All rights reserved.

No part of this book may be reproduced in any form without permission in writing from the publisher, except by a reviewer who may quote brief passages in a review or **for limited educational use**. The trademark "Nomad Press" and the Nomad Press logo are trademarks of Nomad Communications, Inc.

This book was manufactured by CGB Printers, North Mankato, Minnesota, United States
September 2019, Job #280801
ISBN Softcover: 978-1-61930-773-5
ISBN Hardcover: 978-1-61930-770-4

Educational Consultant, Marla Conn

Questions regarding the ordering of this book should be addressed to
Nomad Press
2456 Christian St., White River Junction, VT 05001
www.nomadpress.net
Printed in the United States.

FOSSIL HUNTRESS

Mary Leakey

PALEONTOLOGIST

ANDI DIEHN
Illustrated by Katie Mazeika

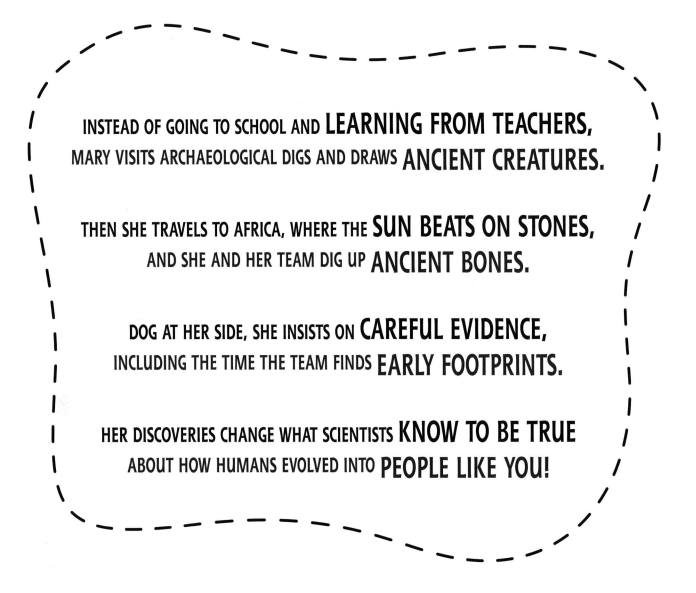

INSTEAD OF GOING TO SCHOOL AND **LEARNING FROM TEACHERS,** MARY VISITS ARCHAEOLOGICAL DIGS AND DRAWS **ANCIENT CREATURES.**

THEN SHE TRAVELS TO AFRICA, WHERE THE **SUN BEATS ON STONES,** AND SHE AND HER TEAM DIG UP **ANCIENT BONES.**

DOG AT HER SIDE, SHE INSISTS ON **CAREFUL EVIDENCE,** INCLUDING THE TIME THE TEAM FINDS **EARLY FOOTPRINTS.**

HER DISCOVERIES CHANGE WHAT SCIENTISTS **KNOW TO BE TRUE** ABOUT HOW HUMANS EVOLVED INTO **PEOPLE LIKE YOU!**

When Mary Leakey was a little girl, she and her father liked to learn about the past. They liked to look at cave paintings. **Mary was fascinated.**

"Why did people paint on rocks?" she wondered.

As she grew up, Mary didn't go to school like other children. She read books about the things that interested her, such as bones from the past. These are called fossils.

Mary became very good at drawing fossils. She wanted to be a paleontologist.

She wanted to learn about the secrets of the past.

When she was older, Mary met a scientist named Louis Leakey. She illustrated a book he was writing and traveled with him to Africa.

ADAM'S ANCESTORS

L.S.B. Leakey

Africa is a land of
sun and heat, and
of zebras, elephants,
and giraffes living
free and wild.

**And it is a land that
holds secrets from
the ancient past.**

Mary wanted to find fossils
and learn all of those secrets.

Africa was where she could learn to be a paleontologist.

She loved the sun and the grasslands all around. She loved the animals that moved across the land.

Most of all, she loved digging in the dirt with Louis and their team of scientists, looking for fossils.

Everyone on the team wrote notes
about the fossils they found.

They described the land where
the fossils were discovered.

They measured, drew, and were
very, very careful with each fossil.

Mary insisted
that everyone
follow
directions and
do careful
scientific work.

In Africa, Mary found a skull that was about 16 million years old.

Rusinga
Island

Lake
Victoria

TANZANIA

She made this important discovery on Rusinga Island in Lake
Victoria. The skull had belonged to the ancestor of an ape.

Lake
Victoria

KENYA

Olduvai
Gorge

TANZANIA

INDIAN
OCEAN

Later, Mary made another discovery at a place
called Olduvai Gorge. She found pieces of bone
that fit together to form part of a skull.

It was part of the head of an early human.

**This skull was almost 2 million years old. It was
the first of its kind ever found in East Africa.**

Years later, in the same part of Africa, Mary and her team discovered animal footprint fossils.

Among the animal tracks, Mary found footprints from early humans!

These early humans are our ancestors. Mary's discovery was important because it showed that our ancestors walked upright on two feet early in our history.

Mary studied these footprint fossils for many years. She worked with lots of other people and always had her dog nearby for company. **She learned many secrets of the past.**

As she got older, kneeling on the ground got harder. Mary decided to stop working in the field. She lived in Africa, the land of sun, grass, and fossils, until she passed away.

Today, Mary's discoveries still inspire paleontologists.

ACTIVITY TIME!

Draw a Specimen!

Illustrations have always been very important in science, especially before there were lots of cameras and computers!

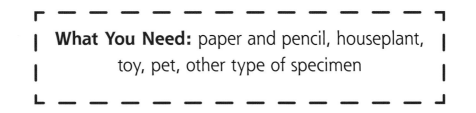

> **What You Need:** paper and pencil, houseplant, toy, pet, other type of specimen

First, closely examine your specimen.

This can be anything you can keep in front of you for a while as you draw it. What kind of texture does your specimen have? What size is it? What shapes does it include?

With your pencil, delicately sketch your specimen on your paper.

Don't worry if your first attempts don't look much like your specimen! The more you draw, the better you'll get.

When you have a sketch you like, add labels to it to show what the different parts of your specimen are. If you want, you can trace over your pencil marks with pen to make it darker.

Add the date and location to every drawing you make so you know where and when you made it!

QUOTE CONNECTIONS!

Try these text-to-text connections!

Can you match Mary's quotes to the moment in the story?

"I never felt interpretation was my job. **What I came to do was to dig things up** and take them out as well as I could."

"I really like to feel that **I am on solid ground**, and that is never solid ground." (referring to interpretation)

"I go once a year to the Serengeti to see the wildebeest migrations **because that means a lot to me**, but I avoid Olduvai if I can because it is a ruin. It is most depressing."

"Fortunately, there is **so much underground still**. It is a vast place, and there is plenty more under the surface **for future generations** that are better educated."

"You know, **you only find what you are looking for**, really, if the truth be known."

TIMELINE

1913 Mary Nicol is born in London on February 6.

1933 Mary meets Louis Leakey at a talk he gives at the Royal Anthropologist Institute.

1935 Mary travels to Africa for the first time.

1936 Mary and Louis marry and work together in Africa.

TIMELINE

1959 Mary finds the oldest early human skull ever discovered.

1972 Mary's husband, Louis, passes away.

1974 Mary begins excavations at a place in Africa called Laetoli.

1978 In a field of hardened ash, Mary's team discovers footprints from early humans. The prints date back 3.6 million years.

1996 Mary Leakey passes away.

GLOSSARY

ancestors: the people who lived before you.

archaeological: having to do with archaeology, the study of ancient people through the objects they left behind.

evolve: a change in a living thing in response to the world around it.

excavate: to dig up or uncover something.

fascinated: strongly attracted and interested.

fossil: the remains of any living thing, including animals and plants, that have been preserved in rock.

grassland: a large area of land covered with grass.

interpret: to think about and explain something.

paleontology: the study of the history of life on Earth through the study of the fossils of plants and animals.

paleontologist: a scientist who studies paleontology by studying plant and animal fossils.

scientist: a person who studies science and asks questions about the natural world, seeking answers based on facts.

specimen: a sample of something, such as a plant or animal.